OTHER BOOKS BY
THEODORE ROSZAK

Nonfiction

Person/Planet

Unfinished Animal

The Cult of Information

Where the Wasteland Ends

The Making of a Counter Culture

Editor and contributor

The Dissenting Academy

Masculine/Feminine
(with coeditor Betty Roszak)

Sources

Fiction

Dreamwatcher

Bugs

Pontifex

FROM SATORI
TO SILICON VALLEY

San Francisco and the American Counterculture

Theodore Roszak

640512

Don't Call It Frisco Press
Publisher & Distributor
4079 19th Avenue
San Francisco
California
94132

DON'T CALL IT FRISCO PRESS
4079 19th Avenue
San Francisco, CA 94132

ISBN: 0-917583-09-4

Copyrights and Acknowledgements:

CITY LIGHTS for "Buddhist Anarchism" by Gary Snyder, Copyright 1962. From *The Journal for the Protection of All Beings,* McClure, Ferlinghetti & Meltzer, editors, City Lights, San Francisco.

DELACORTE PRESS for "All Watched Over by Machines of Loving Grace" by Richard Brautigan, copyright 1968. Excerpted from *The Pill Versus the Springhill Mine Disaster,* reprinted by permission of Delacorte Press/Seymour Lawrence, New York.

DOUBLEDAY & CO. for *Hackers* by Steven Levy, copyright 1984.

PRAEGER PUBLISHERS for quote by Bill Voyd from *Shelter and Society,* edited by Paul Oliver, copyright 1969.

SAN FRANCISCO FOCUS MAGAZINE for quotes from an interview with Stewart Brand in the February 1985 issue.

SAN FRANCISCO ORACLE for quotes from issues #6, 1967, and #12, 1967. Reprinted with permission of Allan Cohen, Editor.

ST. MARTIN'S PRESS for *Buckminster Fuller, An Autobiographical Monologue/Scenario* by Robert Snyder, copyright 1970.

ST. MARTIN'S PRESS for *Children of Prosperity* by Hugh Gardner, copyright 1978.

The Times They Are A-Changing

A shortened version of this essay was presented at San Francisco State University in April 1985 as the Alvin Fine Lecture. A few weeks before the event, a student in the Public Affairs Office called me to arrange some campus publicity. He had a question.

"Where's Satori?"

"What?" I asked.

"It says 'From Satori to Silicon Valley,'" he explained. "I know where Silicon Valley is. But where's Satori?"

"The Zen state of enlightenment ... you never heard of that?"

"Oh. I never took any courses in Oriental religion."

I started to explain the term, spelling out its

once obvious connection with the counterculture of the sixties.

"Counterculture," he interrupted. "That's ... hippies. All like that?"

Suddenly I felt one hundred years old.

I often feel that way these days. I teach students now who have no clear idea what a "sit-in" was ... or a "teach-in". Who no longer remember "the Days of Rage" or "the Summer of Love". Who know Woodstock only as a picture in their textbooks. For whom the Chicago Seven (or was it Eight?) are an unknown quantity. Only to be expected. After all, when I was making my way through college, what did I know about Sacco and Vanzetti ... the Memorial Day Massacre ... the Moscow Trials ...

Time passes. Social memory is a shifting cloud. Kids awkwardly segueing into citizenhood leave ancestral traumas and triumphs behind. Which is as it should be. Provided they go on to their own better things.

Will they?

I decided to attach this little note for readers who also might be uncertain where Satori is.

THE GATHERING OF THE TRIBES

In these days of instant nostalgia, current events pass from journalism into folklore before they have had a decent chance to become history. This is certainly true of the period we call "the sixties". The American counterculture that flourished during that period – from the late fifties to the mid-seventies – has already been assigned a canonical image in the history texts that are now being used in our high schools and colleges. It surfaces there in the penultimate chapter, where the narrative, having swept like a stormy surf across the story of Vietnam and Watergate, begins to ebb sullenly away toward the Carter and Reagan years. The usual depiction is that of high-spirited young people, ungroomed, unkempt, and uncouth, disporting themselves in the open air –

a park, a field, a forest. Their straggly hair streams free or is banded back Indian style. Their clothes are patched, befringed, and beaded – a motley of backwoods disshevelment and barbaric splendor. Often they are loaded with backpacks, bedrolls, stash bags that lend the aura of transiency: people on the road far from home, ready to crash anywhere for the night – in the woods, under the stairs, in the back of the van. Mendicant citizens of the world, pausing to sing or play as they make their way to Berkeley or Boulder, Cambridge or Katmandu, North Beach or the Northwoods. Sometimes, more soberly, they flourish signs: "Make Love not War", "End the Bombing Now", "Give Peace a Chance".

Were there ever such people – really?

For some years now (since about half way through the seventies) I have had the oppressive sense of an embarrassed reluctance on all sides to recall the role that beatniks, hippies, flower children once played in our society. When their period in history is mentioned, we hasten to attach a snide disclaimer, a wised-up dismissal. We peer back through two decades of fickle journalism, national self-doubt, and social backlash, wondering if the dissenting politics of the sixties might simply have been another media fiction. Certainly in recent years, the only flesh and blood examples of the countercultural image I have come across have been the barely surviving casualties of the era that still haunt downtown Berkeley, panhandling for spare change. Their sad squalor is evidence of nothing braver or more inspiring than being bummed out and overaged.

Yet, with a little effort and some candor, I can remember the happier originals of these faded caricatures as they once enlivened the streets of the Haight-Ashbury and Telegraph Avenue. In its time, their persona of ragged independence – or some reasonable facsimile thereof – was a proud and prominent emblem of cultural disaffiliation blossoming in the streets of every major city, on the campus of every minor college and high school. It was a stance that claimed to have broken irrevocably with the urban-industrial culture that ruled the world. The style purported to be "natural", "organic", a principled rejection of antiseptic, upwardly mobile middle-class habits in favor of a return to folk origins and lost traditions. A bit of the bohemian rebel, a bit of the noble savage. Those who assumed the identity spoke of themselves as "freaks" and assembled in hastily improvised and

3

ephemeral "tribes" where simple and funky living was the rule. At the Morning Star Ranch in Marin, the residents called their way of life "voluntary primitivism", a design for living beyond both excessive affluence and minimal hygiene.

For some, the search for a postindustrial alternative led out of the cities to rural communes, few of which were destined to survive. But even in the cities, one could find "collectives" where the ethos was that of urban cave-dwellers, camping out indoors. In Berkeley in the late sixties, when my wife and I were looking for a house to rent, we had occasion to inspect a number of these domestic experiments – or what was left in their wake after the resident tribe had decamped without paying the rent. Musty houses in a state of advanced disrepair where the inhabitants had once pitched tents in the living room or spent the night in sleeping bags. In the kitchens, pantries were filled with stale brown rice and active vermin; in the refrigerators, one might find several months' supply of spoiled groceries and well-sprouted soy cakes. In these quarters, one sensed that organic foods were a sort of talisman, sufficiently potent in their very presence to repeal the germ theory of disease. Also there were the signs of many animals once resident or still haunting the premises – unleashed, unhousebroken, very likely unfed. In the Haight-Ashbury and the East Bay, there was a cult of the "organic dog" – the larger, the less washed and tamed, the better. For a period, there were neighborhoods in Berkeley and San Francisco that took on the look and the fragrance of barnyards or hunting camps.

ORGANIC COMMONWEALTH
AND BUDDHIST ANARCHY

Perhaps the high water mark of this symbolic effort to rusticate western civilization was the brief and turbulent episode in Berkeley remembered as "People's Park". What the Human Be-In in San Franciso of 1967 had been for one day, what the Woodstock Festival in upstate New York in early 1969 had been for a weekend, People's Park was meant to be for keeps. The event might be seen as the culmination of the direct action social philosophy proclaimed by the Haight-Ashbury Diggers. After issuing a series of broadsides in late 1966 that called for an urban anarchist order of life, the Diggers had begun a daily come-one, come-all free food project under the slogan "it's free because it's yours." The food was either stolen or scrounged from merchants around the city (most of it days-old and unsaleable if still edible) and served up for the growing population of young, underfed street people. But history's first Diggers – those of seventeenth century England – had not been panhandlers; they had been would-be revolutionaries. Dispossessed farmers and artisans, they had occupied the land, proclaimed it the "common treasure" of the people, and begun tilling it. (Not much land, actually; there were only a few dozen Diggers. Nor did the occupation last long; only a few months before they were driven off, condemned as madmen rather than criminals.) People's Park in Berkeley 1969 revived that original Digger ideal. A piece of the city's turf had been liberated by some shaggy squatters (and their dogs) from Governor Reagan and the University Regents. Promptly, the word went out for the tribes to pitch their tents, cultivate their gardens, warm their bones by the campfire, and create the Organic Commonwealth. In People's Park, the aboriginals – their history dated back all of several days at most – called themselves "sod brothers" and set about planting crops that never sprouted, and which few would have stayed put long enough to harvest. In any case, the

Governor and the Regents quashed the experiment before it had the chance to fail, leaving it as another emblematic gesture along the way. The history of the period is mainly a collection of such emblems and symbols, evocative but ephemeral.

There were those, however, who took the stalking of the wild asparagus more seriously and put a deal of inventive thought and practical energy into the skills of postindustrial survival. There was, for example, the Portola Institute in Menlo Park, which dates from l966. From it, along a number of routes, one can trace the origins of several ingenious projects in the Bay Area whose aim was to scale-down, democratize, and humanize our hypertrophic technological society. These included the Briarpatch Network, the Farallones Institute, the Integral Urban House, the Simple Living Project. On the national scene, the most visible of these efforts was the *Whole Earth Catalog* of 1968, a landmark publication of the period. *The Catalog* was an exuberant compendium of resourceful possiblities for laid-back, but self-reliant living: wood-burning stoves, home remedies, mail order moccasins, durable tools. I can recall a meeting I attended down the San Francisco peninsula where the first rather ratty-looking edition of the *Catalog* (the print order was about 1000) was handed around the circle hot off the press. It was closely scrutinized with a mixture of wide-eyed wonder and honest glee. For, yes, here were the tools and skills of the alternative folk economy to come, the tribal technology ready to be ordered and put to work. When the cities collapsed (as they were certain to do) and all the supply lines froze up (which might be any day now) these would be the means of cunning survival. Right there for all to see was a blueprint of the world's best tipi. There was even a book available for a modest price that showed how to deliver your own baby in a log cabin.

How many who read the *Catalog* ever ordered its goods or used its advice? I suspect that, for many, it was more the banner of a cause than the real tool it was meant to be. But even if one discounts most of these gestures as impractical whimsey, they stand as a provocative assertion of justified discontent which reached out, however unsteadily, toward organic values that our industrial culture has left far behind. That assertion, so I believe, represented much that was best in America's abbreviated countercultural episode. Somewhere in that longing for an earthier texture of life, there lay the saving sensibility that might have disciplined our runaway industrialism and given it a human face. Certainly we have had no stronger an appetite for social and economic alternatives, no livelier a discussion of major issues facing our high industrial system than we experienced during this brief, superheated interval. What is a sane standard of production and consumption? What is the true wealth of nations? What is the meaning of work, of leisure, of community, of masculinity and femininity, of freedom and fulfillment? What is the relationship of economy to environment? How do we create an economics of permanence? What are the values of a planetary culture?

If the wishful paradigm that sparked discussion of issues like these was a somewhat romanticized neoprimitivism, that may be of less intellectual importance than the quality of the ideas that soon found currency within this unlikely public of dissenting and dropped-out middle class youth. For these included the human-scaled economics (sometimes quaintly called the "Buddhist economics") of E.F. Schumacher, the communitarian philosophy of Paul Goodman and Murray Bookchin, the feminist insurgency of the women's movement, the convivial social theories of Ivan Illych, the ecological poetics of Gary Snyder, the manifold insights of the humanistic and human potential psychologies. Like so many tributaries, these currents of thought at last flowed into the environmental movement of the early seventies, which survives as the most durable offshoot of countercultural protest.

Permeating all these issues was a peculiarly west coast American reading of Zen-Taoist nature mysticism, a reborn sense of allegiance to the Earth and its rhythms which centered especially in the postwar Bay Area. The positive side of youthful disaffiliation during the sixties was the discovery of a new postindustrial standard of wealth and well-being that borrowed heavily upon oriental philosophy. I have met academic specialists who insist that even Alan Watts, who did so much to popularize Zen, did not grasp the authentic meaning of satori. So it would be hazardous to say how many members of the untutored counterculture achieved a studied knowledge of this elusive tradition. But many had at least acquired from these exotic sources an awareness of values that commanded no respect in the mainstream of our frenzied industrial economy: a trust in the organism and the spontaneous patterns of nature, a sense of right livelihood, a taste for pleasures of the senses and splendors of the mind that money cannot buy nor machines produce. The learnedness may not always have been there, but the longing was. And sometimes timely intuition supplies what scholarship cannot provide. If the raggle-taggle youth of the sixties had any guiding star before them, I think it was the hobo Taoist saints and shabby Zen masters, civilization's original anarchist philosophers who taught the art of living lightly on the Earth. Young and raw as the counterculture may have been, there were those in its ranks who recognized the relevance of that tradition to the needs of a culture sunk over its eyes in an obsessive struggle to conquer nature, to obliterate all traditional wisdom in the name of "progress", to transform the planet into an industrial artifact. They perceived the nuclear death-wish that lies at the core of that Promethean obsession and, accordingly, they proposed a more becoming human alternative.

One of the earliest and strongest statements of the ideal can be found in Gary Snyder's terse manifesto "Buddhist Anarchism". It appears in the *Journal for the Protection of All Beings,* another landmark publication of the era, this one issued by

Lawrence Ferlinghetti's City Lights Books in 1961.

Modern America has become economically dependent on a fantastic system of stimulation of greed which cannot be fulfilled, sexual desire which cannot be satiated, and hatred which has no outlet except against oneself or the persons one is supposed to love. The conditions of the cold war have turned all modern societies, Soviet included, into hopeless brain-stainers, creating populations of *"preta"* – hungry ghosts – with giant appetites and throats no bigger than needles. The soil, and forests, and all animal life are being wrecked to feed these cancerous mechanisms.

The disaffiliation and acceptance of poverty by practicing Buddhists becomes a positive force. The traditional harmlessness and refusal to take life in any form has nation-shaking implications. The practice of meditation, for which one needs "only the ground beneath one's feet" wipes out mountains of junk being pumped into the mind by "communications" and super-market universities. The belief in a serene and generous fulfillment of natural desires … destroys arbitary frustration-creating customs and points the way to a kind of community that would amaze moralists and eliminate armies of men who are fighters because they cannot be lovers.[1]

A TASTE FOR INDUSTRIAL
LIGHT AND MAGIC

But now, if we were to fix upon this one aspect of the counterculture – its mystic tendencies and principled funkiness – we would not be doing justice to the deep ambiguity of the movement. We would be overlooking the allegiance it maintained – for all its vigorous dissent – to a certain irrepressible Yankee ingenuity, a certain world-beating American fascination with making and doing. For along one important line of descent, it is within this same population of rebels and drop-outs that we can find the inventors and entrepreneurs who helped lay the foundations of the California computer industry. The connections between these two seemingly contra-dictory aspects of the movement are fascinating to draw out and ponder – especially since both wings of the conterculture came to be more fully unfolded here in the San Francisco Bay Area than any place else. This is where the Zen-Taoist impulse arose and found (for example, in the San Francisco Zen Center) its most studied expression in America; this is where the mendicant-communitarian lifestyle, both urban and rural, found its main public examples; this is where the new ecological sensibility first announced its presence and first organized its political energies. And this is where the inspired young hackers who would revolutionize Silicon Valley gathered in their greatest numbers.

The truth is, if one probes just beneath the surface of the bucolic hippy image, one finds this puzzling infatuation with certain forms of outré technology reaching well back into the early sixties. I first became aware of its presence when I realized that the countercultural students I knew during that period were almost exclusively, if not maniacally, readers of science fiction. They were reading more of the genre than the publishers could provide. Side by side with the appeal of folk music and primitive ways, handicrafts and organic husbandry, there was a childlike, Oh Wow! confabulation with the spaceships and miraculous mechanisms that would make Stanley Kubrick's *2001* and the television series *Star Trek* cult favorites, and which would eventually produce the adult audience for (and the producers of) *Star Wars* in the later seventies and eighties. The same eyes that were scanning the tribal past for its wonders and amazements were also on the look-out for the imagined marvels of what the San Francisco filmmaker George Lucas would one day call "Industrial Light and Magic".

Similarly, if we turn back to the *Whole Earth Catalog,* we can find the same hybrid taste. Alongside the rustic skills and tools, we discover high industrial techniques and instruments: stereo systems, cameras, cinematography, and, of course, computers. On one page the "Manifesto of the Mad Farmer Liberation Front" (Wendell Berry's plea for family-scaled organic agriculture); on the next, Norbert Wiener's cybernetics. I recall how this juxtaposition jarred when I first noticed it. But then I thought again and tried to restrain my doubts. There was, after all, something charming about the blithe eclecticism of this worldview. Granted that a catalog is by its very nature a melange. But this catalog clearly meant to project a consistent vision. It seemed to be saying that

17

all human ingenuity deserved to be celebrated –
from the stone axe and American Indian medicine to
modern electronics. Clearly, in so saying, the
Catalog spoke for an audience that wanted to see
things that way. Or rather, the *Catalog* found the
voices that could do that job. And of all the voices to
which it gave a forum, none was to become more
prominent than Buckminster Fuller, the man who in-
formed a generation that it was already on board a
spaceship called Planet Earth, and who presumed to
write its "operating manual".

Now, Buckminster Fuller had a long, long
career. His prefabricated Dymaxion House of the
late twenties (also called "the four dimensional living machine") dates back to the grandparents of the
countercultural generation. From that point forward, his life story went through many ups and
downs; but there can be no question that the sixties
(when Fuller was in his seventies) were his zenith.
Not only did he make the front cover of *Time*
magazine (in 1964) but he became one of the prophetical voices of the American counterculture –
starting with a prolonged campus residency at San
Jose State College that brought him to the Bay Area
in early 1966. Thanks to that appearance and subse-

quently to the prominence Stewart Brand gave him in the *Whole Earth Catalog*, Fuller was launched on the final and most spectacular phase of his career. On the first page of the *Catalog*, the full corpus of Fuller's works was generously presented under the inscription: "the insights of Buckminster Fuller initiated this catalog." From that point forward, Fuller became the necessary presence at New Age conferences, symposia, and workshops: a sort of peripatetic global wizard who might tie his awe-inspired audience down for four or five hours at a stretch while he recited the history of the universe.

What was it that made this odd figure so remarkably influential in countercultural circles? In part, it may have been his grandfatherly persona, which appealed to young people in search of wise elders and finding so few. In part, too, it might have had to do with his maverick image, that of the outcast genius scorned by the schools and the professionals, and so becoming the senior drop-out who could speak to junior drop-outs. But one must add to this his unique talent for self-advertisement, his capacity, by way of grandiloquent obfuscation, to make much out of little: little ideas, little inventions that could be sensationally clothed in cosmic preten-

sions. If Fuller was half Tom Swift, he was also half
P.T. Barnum. And just as Barnum could turn a not
very special midget or an overaged elephant into
wonders of the world, so Fuller was able to parley a
few modest pieces of eccentric engineering into
achievements of supposedly epoch-making genius –
at least in the eyes of an audience that was in the
market for technological astonishments.

But above all, it was Fuller's worldview that
caught the temper of the time and the movement.
While impishly dissenting in tone, he was up-beat in
spirit: hopeful, sassy, inspirational almost to the
point of euphoria. Fuller was, as one biographer
calls him, a "raging optimist". I must confess that,
though I shared a few platforms with Fuller and did
my best to appreciate his books, I never came across
anything he said that managed to be, at one and the
same time, original, true, significant, and under-
standable. Worse still, I was never able to distinguish his optimism from plain egomania; I would
not have been suprised to hear him announce that he
had invented a better tree. Yet, again and again, I
saw him send audiences away glowing with hope
and resolution. That peculiar magic made Fuller and
his Bay Area disciples the major spokesmen for a

philosophy of postindustrial life that has done much to shape the style and expectations of the computer industry, especially as it has grown up in Silicon Valley over the past ten years.

REVERSIONARIES AND TECHNOPHILES

I should explain how I am using the term "post-industrial" here. I mean it in the sense that would supposedly place us permanently beyond the chronic failures of the industrial societies: the instability of boom and bust, the waste of life and resources, the injustice and brutality. In its postindustrial phase, our society would not simply have matured but transcended, reaching that point where our technological genius would at last have freed us from the tyranny of getting and spending, compulsive productivity and frantic consumption, mass manipulation and military necessity so that we might live a fully human life. "Postindustrial" indicates a stage of moral, not economic, growth.

That utopian goal has been with us since the first appearance of the Dark Satanic Mills. But in the western world, the vision of our postindustrial future has been polarized between two very different scenarios: that of the "reversionaries" and that of the "technophiles".

For the *reversionaries,* who trace back to John Ruskin, William Morris, and the Romantic artists generally, industrialism is the extreme state of a cultural disease that must be cured before it kills us. It is a stage of pathological overdevelopment in the history of human economy from which a healthy technology – usually seen as some form of communitarian handicrafts – will have to be salvaged once the industrial system has reached the point of terminal inhumanity. The reversionaries are what Paul Goodman would have called "neolithic conservatives". They look forward to the day when the factories and heavy machinery will be left to molder, and we will have the chance to return to the world of the village, the farm, the hunting camp, the tribe. This would lead us to a life close to the soil and the elements that needs only simple and communal pleasures to find fulfillment. This is the route that, for example, Stephen Gaskin chose for himself

23

and his followers when they left the Experimental College at San Francisco State University in 1971.

Through the middle and later sixties, Gaskin, a former assistant to San Francisco State Professor S.I. Hayakawa, had been teaching a "Monday Night Class" in the student-financed and controlled Experimental College. When the class began to draw some several hundred students, it moved for a brief period to Glide Memorial Church downtown and identified itself as a "religion", with Gaskin as its guru. Finally in late 1971, Gaskin organized a mass exodus via bus caravan that made its way to a 1700 acre farm in Tennessee. The philosophy of the settlement was simple living and "guaranteed good karma". Some have identified Gaskin's following of reconstructed urbanites as "voluntary peasants". Gaskin puts it this way:

> What we are really into is making a living in a clean way. I guess farming is about the cleanest way to make a living. It's just you and the dirt and God. And the dirt – you can't make friends with an acre of ground and get it to give you an "A" like in college or something. If you make friends with it,

you have to put work into it, and then it'll
come back and feed you, it'll really do it.
But you can't snow it or anything like that
– it's going to be real with you.[2]

The result of Gaskin's philosophy in application was
to be one of the few long-term communitarian ven-
tures to come out of the sixties. By dint of hard
work, fraternal sharing, and minimal consumption,
The Farm managed to prosper into the 1980's on a
regimen of soybeans and natural childbirth.

Over against this strategem of radical with-
drawal and reversion, we have the *technophiliac vision* of our industrial destiny, a modern tradition of
thought that links back to the likes of Saint-Simon,
Robert Owen, and H.G. Wells. For these utopian in-
dustrialists, as for Buckminster Fuller after them,
the cure for our industrial ills will not be found in
things past, but in Things To Come. Indeed, it will
be found at the climax of the industrial process.
What is required, therefore, is not squeamish reversion, but brave perseverance. We must adapt re-
sourcefully to industrialism as a necessary stage of
social evolution, monitoring the process with a cunning eye for its life-saving potentialities. As we

approach the crisis that threatens calamity, we must grasp these opportunities as they emerge and use them to redeem the system from within. The way out of our dilemma is to tunnel fearlessly through until we reach daylight.

One recognizes at once the familiar Marxist pattern of history in this vision. As against the utopian visionaries who would abscond from industrial society, Marx insisted that the logic of history had to be worked through in its proper phases: from feudalism to capitalism, from capitalism to socialism, from socialism to communism. But one also notices that in Fuller's foreshortened version of the philosophy, we are dealing with the views of a technician, not a political economist. In sharp contrast to Marx, Fuller is a sociological illiterate. There is simply no political context to his thought. Instead, where Marx deals in class conflict and political power, Fuller offers us ... *inventions*. The industrial system produces inventions, and the inventions are simply to be appropriated by clever engineers like Fuller and used to save the human race. The inventions make possible things their capitalist owners cannot envision. But mavericks like Fuller, purporting to stand outside the system, recognize these possibilities and hasten to take advantage of them. As Fuller put it:

> The individual can take initiative without anybody's permission. Only individuals can...look for the principles manifest in their experience that others may be overlooking because they are too preoccupied with how to please some boss or with how to earn money. ...The individual is the only one who could think in a cosmically adequate manner.[3]

Thus, these "individuals" outsmart and outflank the high and the mighty, who, one is left to conclude, simply surrender to their superior insight.

What is an example of such a clever gambit? Well, Fuller was a man of one example, the invention he always fell back on to prove every point: the geodesic dome, on which he held the patent. Had not advanced engineering and industrial technology made this stupendous invention possible? And was not the whole history of the world going to be transformed by the dome? QED.

There was a cult of the geodesic dome during

the sixties. It began with the popular domebooks of San Francisco architect Lloyd Kahn, who was converted to domesmanship by Fuller when the inventor came to the San Francisco Bay Area. Thanks to Kahn's books and the *Whole Earth Catalog*, the hope sprang up that communities of domes might blossom overnight outside major cities – like barbarian encampments embodying the new postindustrial culture. (As far as I'm aware, the closest approach to that goal was Drop City near Trinidad Colorado, a "weed patch commune" whose several funky structures were rigged up out of salvaged junk from the nearest city dump.) The dome quickly became more than an architectural eccentricity; it came to symbolize a new, worldwide style of shelter which combined the values of simplicity, economy, durability, communalism, and whose tetrahedron units had (so Fuller insisted) tapped the deep geometrical logic of the cosmos.

Fuller's followers were quick to take his claims for the dome at full value. As one of the founders of Drop City pronounced:

To live in a dome is – psychologically – to be in closer harmony with natural struc-

28

ture. Macrocosm and microcosm are recreated, both the celestial sphere and molecular and crystalline forms.

Cubical buildings are structurally weak and uneconomic. Corners constrict the mind. Domes break into new dimensions. They help to open man's perception and expand his approaches to creativity. The dichotomy between utilitarian and aesthetic, between artist and layman is broken down.[4]

Another dome missionary proclaimed:

Soon domed cities will spread across the world, anywhere land is cheap – on the deserts, in the swamps, on mountains, tundras, ice caps. The tribes are moving, building completely free and open way stations, each a warm and beautiful conscious environment. We are winning.[5]

Now there were a number of problems with domes. Most of them, even those built in the deserts, the swamps, the mountains, had to have their struts and shafts and connectors, their plywood and fiberglass, shipped in from some distant industrial metropolis. And none of them were all that much cheaper or easier to build than a quonset hut or a Butler barn. And most of them leaked, unless they were shielded by a vast and fragile plastic skin – again imported from the metropolis. And none could be insulated unless they were sprayed or coated with an industrial chemical. And none of them in style or structural substance ever bore any respectful relationship to their locality. Indeed, the dome was designed by its maker to be placeless, meant to be plunked down anywhere from the arctic to the tropics as an assertion of the global industrial dominance. But none of this seemed to matter to the dome enthusiasts; by virtue of Fuller's intoxicating rhetoric and boundless optimism, the dome was seen as an icon of our social salvation.

Fuller was not alone in extrapolating the technophiliac vision of postindustrial history. There were others, each of whom became, at some point, a countercultural favorite. There was Marshall McLuhan, who saw the electronic media as the secret of building a new "global village" that was somehow cozy, participative, and yet at the same time technologically sophisticated. There was Paolo Soleri, who believed that the solution to the ecological crisis of the modern world was the building of megastructural "arcologies" – beehive cities in which the urban billions could be compacted into totally artificial environments. There was Gerard O'Neill, who barnstormed the country whipping up enthusiasm for one of the zaniest schemes of all: the launching of self-contained space colonies for the millions. For a few years, O'Neill became a special fascination of Stewart Brand and the *Whole Earth Catalog* (later *The Co-Evolution Quarterly*). In each of these cases, one sees the same assumption brought into play: the industrial process, pushed to its limit, generates its own best medicine. Out of the advanced research of the electronics, plastics, chemical, and aerospace industries, there emerge solutions to all our political and environmental problems.

MACHINES OF LOVING GRACE

This is the familiar scenario of technophiliac utopianism. But now we come upon something new – and puzzling. For there were those in the ranks of the counterculture who sought to work an odd variation on the futuristic theme. *They insisted they could have it both ways:* the best of high tech, the best of the Haight-Ashbury lifestyle … together. The technophiliac route forward would lead to a reversionary future. When H.G. Wells envisioned Things To Come, he saw a gleamingly sterile urban world run by a benevolent technocratic elite. But for many in the counterculture, the result of high industrial technology would be something like a tribal democracy where the citizenry might still be dressed in buckskin and go berry-picking in the woods. The artificial environment made *more* artificial would somehow become more ... natural. Thus, the odd mix of rustic savvy and advanced technology displayed in the pages of the *Whole Earth Catalog* was not confusion but synthesis. The motto of the philosophy might almost have been "Forward... to the Neolithic!"

At times, this synthesis seemed to stem from nothing more than some very slippery metaphors. For example, McLuhan's conception of the urbanized mass media, pressed to its extreme, becomes a "village". For O'Neill, the space rocket and satellite, developed on a gargantuan scale, return us to a "frontier": the *high* frontier, which, its enthusiasts seemed to think, would be something like the world of the log cabin and wood-burning stove. The fans who organized the L-5 Society to promote O'Neill's ideas liked to imagine vistas of homesteads and organic gardens inside their orbiting steel canisters, plus no end of weightless fun and games sky-diving and windsurfing in zero gravity. Even Soleri's human antheaps were seen as a way of preserving the wilderness in its pristine condition – though one can only shudder at the prospect of the tens of thousands of arcological tenants lined up at every elevator shaft in the structure, waiting to get to the picnic grounds.

I can offer a striking personal example of this strange amalgamation of reversionary and techno-philiac values in action. Somewhere in the mid-seventies, one of the New Age religious groups – it was Yogi Bhajan's 3HO (the Holy, Healthy, Happy Organization, a transplanted Indian Sikh group) – invited me to participate in a "planetary symposium" that would be held simultaneously in three major cities. (Buckminster Fuller would, of course, be the keynote speaker.) The themes of the event would be such staple countercultural values as economic simplicity ("Small is Beautiful"), ecological sanity, spiritual fulfillment, participative democracy. It would be a sort of planet-sized Woodstock. But how would it all be held together, I asked. The answer was: by continuous, day-and-night telecommunications coverage broadcast via satellite and projected on giant video screens in each city. The global village would at last have been realized. Yielding to my usual Luddite instincts, I suggested that such means might conflict with the desired end. My doubts were met with blank incomprehension, but they only deepened when the entire event was finally delegated to a production crew from Walt Disney

enterprises. As it turned out, the cost of the technology finally overwhelmed the modest budget available, reduced the symposium to a fiasco, and
bankrupted its organizers.

The personal computer might be seen as another example of this wishful alliance of the reversionary and technophiliac visions. Once again, we have
the same mix of homespun and high tech. After all,
in its early days, home computer invention and
manufacturing did resemble a sort of primitive
cottage industry. The work could be done out of
attics and garages with simple means and lots of
brains. The people pioneering the enterprise were
cut from the mold of the Bucky Fuller maverick:
talented drop-outs going their own way and clearly
outflanking the lumbering giants of the industry,
beating them to the punch with a *people's* computer.

For that matter, even before the personal
computer had matured into a marketable commod-
ity, there were idealistic young hackers who wanted
to rescue the computer from the corporations for
radical political uses. The earliest effort of this kind
in the United States was Resource One, the creation
of a group of Berkeley computer folk who had come
together during the Cambodian crisis of Spring

1970. Distressed at the near monopoly of computer power by the government and the major corporations, this small band of disgruntled computer scientists set about building a people's information service. By 1971 they had managed to acquire a retired XDS-940 timeshare computer from the Transamerica Corporation and had quartered it in the Project One warehouse-community on Howard Street, south of Market in San Francisco, where they hoped it might be used by political activists to compile mailing lists, coordinate voter surveys, and serve as an all-purpose social-economic database. Resource One was never a great success, perhaps in part because, by the time it got under way, many radical hackers had transferred their hopes to the new generation of compact, more affordable microcomputers, which seemed to be a more practical way to democratize information.

But before its demise, Resource One had transmuted into a form of computer street politics; it had become the project called Community Memory. Community Memory's aim was to locate free computer terminals in public places – like the Mission branch library in San Francisco or Leopold's Record Store in Berkeley – where they could be used as a totally open, unexpurgated people's electronic bulletin board. This effort was launched by a parent company called Loving Grace Cybernetics. Its title was taken from a poem by Richard Brautigan which captures perfectly the much-prized synthesis of reversionary and technophiliac values.

> I like to think (and
> the sooner the better!)
> of a cybernetic meadow
> where mammals and computers
> live together in mutually
> programming harmony
> like pure water
> touching clear sky
>
> I like to think
> (right now, please!)
> of a cybernetic forest
> filled with pines and electronics
> where deer stroll peacefully
> past computers
> as if they were flowers
> with spinning blossoms

i like to think
(it has to be!)
of a cybernetic ecology
where we are free of our labors
and joined back to nature,
returned to our mammal
brothers and sisters,
and all watched over
by machines of loving grace[6]

Throughout the later seventies, many of the inventors and entrepreneurs-to-be of the rising personal computer industry were meeting along the San Francisco peninsula in funky town meetings where high-level technical problems and solutions could be swapped like backwoods lore over the cracker barrel of the general store. They adopted friendly, folksy names for their early efforts like the Itty Bitty Machine Company (an alternative IBM), or Kentucky Fried Computers, or the Homebrew Computer Club. Stephen Wozniak was one of the regulars at Homebrew, and when he looked around for a name to give his brainchild, he came up with a quaintly soft, organic identity that significantly changed the hard-edged image of high tech: the

Apple. One story has it that the name was chosen by Steven Jobs in honor of the fruitarian diet he had brought back from his journey to the mystic East. The name also carried with it an echo of the old Beatles spirit. And, in an effort to keep that spirit alive, Apple made the last heroic attempt to stage a big, outdoor rock gathering: the US Festivals of 1982 and 1983, on which Wozniak spent $20 million of his own money.

For the surviving remnants of the counterculture in the late seventies, it was digital data, rather than domes, arcologies, or space colonies, that would bring us to the postindustrial promised land. The personal computer would give the millions access to the databases of the world, which – so the argument went – was what they needed in order to become a self-reliant citizenry. The home computer terminal became the centerpiece of a sort of electronic populism. Computerized networks and bulletin boards would keep the tribes in touch, exchanging the vital data that the power elite was denying them. Clever hackers would penetrate the classified databanks that guarded corporate secrets and the mysteries of state. Who would have predicted it? By way of IBM's video terminals, AT&T's phone lines,

Pentagon space shots, and Westinghouse communications satellites, a worldwide, underground community of computer-literate rebels would arise, armed with information and ready to overthrow the technocratic centers of authority; they might even outlast the total collapse and reversion of the high industrial system that had invented their technology. Surely one of the zaniest expressions of the guerrilla hacker worldview was that of Lee Felsenstein, a founder of the Homebrew Computer Club and of Community Memory, later the designer of the Osborne portable computer. Felsenstein's technological style – emphasizing simplicity and resourceful recycling – arose from an apocalyptic vision of the industrial future that might have come straight out of *A Canticle for Liebowitz*. He worked from the view

> that the industrial infrastructure might be snatched away at any time, and the people should be able to scrounge parts to keep their machines going in the rubble of the devastated society; ideally, the machine's design would be clear enough to allow users to figure out where to put those parts.[7]

40

As Felsenstein once put it, "I've got to design so you can put it together out of garbage cans."

It is important to appreciate the political idealism that underlay the home computer in its early days, and to recognize its link with tendencies that were part of the counterculture from the beginning. It is quite as important to recognize that the reversionary-technophiliac synthesis it symbolizes is as naive as it is idealistic. So much so that one feels the need of probing deeper to discover the secret of its strange cogency. For how could anyone believe something so unlikely?

THE SHORT CUT TO SATORI

If we delve a bit further into the origins of the counterculture – back to the late fifties and early sixties – we find what may be the most significant connection between the reversionary and technophiliac wings of the movement. In the beginning, there was the music – always the major carrier of the movement: folk, then rock and roll, then rock in all its permutations. Early on, the music, as it was performed in concert and in the new clubs of the period, took on a special mode of presentation. Its power came from electronic amplification; it borrowed from the apparatus. As grungy as the rock audience may have been, it wanted its music explosively amplified and expertly modulated; it wanted to hear the beat through its pores. Therefore, the music needed machines. In this form, with nothing added, rock was supposedly sufficient to produce mindblowing results. "By itself," the San Francisco psychedelic philosopher Chester Anderson proclaimed

> without the aid of strobe lights, day-glo paints, and other subimaginative copouts, rock engages the entire sensorium, appealing to the intelligence with no interference from the intellect. ...Rock is a tribal phenomenon and constitutes what may be called a twentieth century magic. ...Rock is creating the social rituals of the future.[8]

But soon enough, the audience wanted even more. It wanted ecstasies for the eye as well as the ear. Hence the light shows that began in San Francisco and, in the course of the middle sixties, rapidly became an adjunct of rock performances across the country.

The first light shows performed in the United States were developed as a fine art at San Francisco State College in the early fifties. In 1952, Professor

Seymour Locks staged a highly ambitious three-projector show with live music to inaugurate the school's new Creative Arts Building where a national conference of art educators was being hosted. Professor Locks, together with other members of the San Francisco State art department, went on to pioneer a sizeable repertory of liquid projection and colored light techniques through the later fifties; by the start of the next decade, the new art form was being reworked by many hands, but nowhere more daringly than in the San Francisco rock clubs. There the light shows, augmented by strobe lights and phosphorescent colors, were more than an aesthetic medium; they had been seized upon at once as a way of reproducing and/or occasioning psychedelic experience. They were the visual signature of dope. And from the very outset, the premier dope of the era, LSD, was itself a technology, a laboratory product, the result of advanced research at the Swiss pharmaceutical house of Sandoz and Company.

In the early postwar period, LSD and other laboratory hallucinogens belonged to a small, elite public, made up primarily of top-dollar psychiatrists and their high-society clientele. At that time, before LSD had acquired a criminal aura and had been outlawed, mainstream publications like *Time* and *Life* were prepared to publicize its many therapeutic benefits. But by the early sixties, the hallucinogens had found another, less respectable public; they were being touted among the beat poets and dropped-out kids in the streets of Haight-Ashbury and Greenwich Village as the salvation of our troubled culture. Soon Timothy Leary was proselytizing for dope across America; in the Bay Area, as of 1966, Ken Kesey and his Merry Pranksters were blithely dosing whole audiences on this mysterious elixir (or promising to do so) at the Acid Tests and at the Trips Festival.

The assumption underlying these mass distribution efforts was blunt and simple: *dope saves your soul.* Like the Catholic sacraments, it takes effect *ex opere operato* – by its very ministration. Once this promise crossed wires with the growing interest in oriental mysticism, the psychedelics had been launched as a cultural force. It seemed clear that the research laboratories of the western world – including those of the giant pharmaceutical corporations – had presented the world with a substitute for the age-old spiritual disciplines of the East. Instead of a lifetime of structured contemplation, a few drops of homebrewed acid on a vitamin pill would do the trick. It was the short cut to satori.

"Better Things For Better Living Through Chemistry" ran the slogan of the Dupont Company. And thousands of acidheads were ready to agree. They had heard the music; they had seen the colored lights; they had sampled the dope. Nothing did more to tilt the counterculture toward a naive technophilia than this seductive trio of delights. If the high tech of the western world could offer so great a spiritual treasure, then why not more?

Here, I suspect, is the reason why Buckminster Fuller, Marshall McLuhan, and the other technophiliac utopians struck such a responsive chord among the countercultural young. Acid and rock had prepared an audience for their message, and prepared it in an especially persuasive way that undercut the cerebral levels. For the psychedelics are a powerful, even a shattering experience. Combined with the music and the lights in a total assault upon the senses, they can indeed make anything seem possible. They induce a sense of grandeur and a euphoria that may make the grimmest political realities seem like paper tigers. At the same time, the experience connects – or so its proselytizers always insisted – with primordial mystical powers of the mind that still flourish, or *might* still flourish, in exotic quarters of the globe, among native practitioners and traditional peoples like Carlos Casteneda's legendary Don Juan. This experience, purchased out of the laboratories of our industrial culture, somehow allies its disciples with the ancient, the primitive, the tribal. Its proper use is among huddled comrades, gathered in a sacramental hush in park or field, on the beach, in the wilderness, or the enfolding darkness of an urban den. Here, then, we find the same striking blend of the sophisticated-scientific and the natural-communal that Buckminster Fuller claimed for the geometry of the geodesic dome, and that the Silicon Valley hackers would eventually claim for the personal computer. "This generation absolutely swallowed computers whole, just like dope," Stewart Brand observed in a 1984 interview.[9] There may be more literal truth to the metaphor than he intended.

THE LIGHT THAT FAILED?

With the benefit of hindsight, one can easily see the pathos of the reversionary-technophiliac synthesis – though I think more than a little of it still survives among the computer enthusiasts. The reversionary and the technophiliac choices with which our society confronts us do not so readily combine; indeed, I suspect there is an insurmountable hostility between the large scale technology on which the computer industry is based and the traditional values that the counterculture wished to salvage. The military-industrial complex battens off the giganticism of advanced technology; it is not the ally of communal or organic values. Nor are the corporate leaders of the industrial world so easily outsmarted and outflanked as the Fullerite technophiles always wanted to believe. Moneyed elites are no slouches when it comes to defending their interests. They can outspend their opposition; they can outwait and outwit their enemies by hiring the brains they need as well as the brute power.

It is sad in the extreme to know, as we now do, that, before Ken Kesey and Timothy Leary brought the gospel of LSD to the streets, the CIA had long since undertaken an exhaustive run of experiments with the hallucinogens using human beings as guinea pigs to explore the possibilities of mind control. Similarly, it now seems abundantly clear that long before the personal computer has the chance to restore democratic values, the major corporations and the security agencies of the world will have used the technology to usher in a new era of advanced surveillance and control. As for the space rocket and satellite, we can be sure that by the time the L-5 Society has raised the funds for its first modest colony, the military will already be encamped on the high frontier armed with unheard-of genocidal weaponry.

It was an attractive hope that the high technology of our society might be wrested from the grip of benighted forces and used to restore us to an idyllic natural state. And for a brief moment – while the music swelled, and the lights flashed, and the dope cast its spell – it looked like the road forward to many bright spirits. But ultimately – and really in very short order – the synthesis crumbled, and the technophiliac values of the counterculture won out. They are, after all, the values of the mainstream and the commanding heights, forces that have proved far more tenacious than most members of the counter-culture guessed.

Does this mean that the reversionary wing of the movement was simply a light that failed? In one sense, obviously yes. The urban-industrial domi-nance is more tightly locked to the planet than ever; the search for viable alternatives has gone into a deep eclipse. But a light that fails is still better than un-challenged darkness. For besides winning, there is also being right. And on another level where the historical clock measures out its story in millenia not minutes, the reversionaries may be regarded as prophetical voices that, though largely unheeded, spoke truth to power. Not all that the reversionaries stood for was born from a naive infatuation with simple cultures and native peoples. Besides looking back with fondness, they also looked forward. As

Allen Ginsberg did when he spoke of the Beat poets as the world's Distant Early Warning System. And what he saw ahead made the neoprimitivism of the sixties more a matter of desperate animal survival than charming nostalgia: The death – slow or sudden, by fire or blight – of a civilization grown tragically estranged from the mothering Earth. Our imperial cities turning feral, crumbling beneath the weight of their own arrogance. The lordly power of our machines humbled. The wildness reclaiming its planetary preeminence, perhaps not gently. The bad end of a Faustian bargain that was signed when the first pyramid was raised.

A VISION BOTH BRIGHT AND DARK

The San Francisco poet Lew Welch captured the dark side of the reversionary vision, in his rhapsodic manifesto *Final City/ Tap City.*

Dome of foul air full of radio squeaks and TV signals, foulness flowing into the very waters that made them come to be.

Inside millions of terrified Beings scurry about through senseless mazes of tunnels and lanes. The noise is unendurable. Every sense is insulted. Everybody rushing about on some incomprehensible errand someone forced him to do at pain of death.

...Designed to protect everyone inside from everything outside, ...gradually there was no "outside". Lots of danger, in.

Now these things, Cities, kept getting bigger and bigger and faster and faster, the people getting more and more crazed.

...Leads to Final City, Tap City, any one of a dozen ways. ...You don't even have to figure the Atom Bomb.

City is so Human. It may well be our tragic flaw, seeing City as our Mindless Evolution, irreversible, Man's way of changing, not Biological?

We face great holocausts, terrible catastrophies, all American cities burned from within, and without.

Mercifully, the poet allows his vision to brighten before it passes, confident that the Earth forgives and restores. So let us hope.

However, our beautiful Planet will germinate, underneath this thin skin of City the green will come back to crack these sidewalks. The stinking air will blow away at last, the bays flow clean.

…In the meantime, stay healthy, there are hundreds of miles to walk and work. Keep your mind. We will need it. …Learn the berries, the nuts, the fruit, the small animals and plants. Learn water.

For there must be good men and women in the mountains, and on the beaches, in all the neglected beautiful places, that one day we come back to ghostly cities and set them right, at last.

…In all that rubble, think of the beautiful trinkets we can wave above our heads as we dance![10]

I confess to being baffled by those who think that vision – both the dark and the bright of it – has somehow lost its place on the political agenda.

Perhaps, distracted by media figments and the daily delusions of news, we have lost the ability to distinguish between fashion and fate.

NOTES:

1. Gary Snyder, "Buddhist Anarchism," *Journal for the Protection of All Beings*, City Lights Books, San Francisco, 1961.

2. *Resurgence*, No. 59, Nov.-Dec., 1976, London, p.12.

3. Robert Snyder, *Buckminster Fuller, An Autobiographical Monologue/Scenario*, St. Martin's Press, New York, 1970, p.38.

4. Bill Voyd, "Drop City", in Theodore Roszak, ed. *Sources*, Harper & Row, New York, 1972, p. 276.

5. Hugh Gardner, *Children of Prosperity*, St. Martin's Press, New York, 1978, p.37.

6. Steven Levy, *Hackers*, Doubleday, New York, 1984, p. 169-170.

7. *Hackers*, p. 251.

8. *San Francisco Oracle*, No. 6, 1967.

9. *San Francisco Focus Magazine*, Feb.1985, p. 107.

10. *San Francisco Oracle*, No. 12, 1967.